INJUN

[**Also by Jordan Abel**]

The Place of Scraps
Un/inhabited

Published by Talonbooks

INJUN

JORDAN ABEL

Talonbooks

Talonbooks
9259 Shaughnessy Street, Vancouver, British Columbia, Canada V6P 6R4
www.talonbooks.com

Fourth printing: 2019

Typeset in Minion
Printed and bound in Canada on 100% post-consumer recycled paper

Cover design by Typesmith
Cover photograph by Rebecca Belmore
Interior design by Jordan Abel

Talonbooks acknowledges the financial support of the Canada Council for the Arts, the Government of Canada through the Canada Book Fund, and the Province of British Columbia through the British Columbia Arts Council and the Book Publishing Tax Credit.

Library and Archives Canada Cataloguing in Publication

Abel, Jordan, 1985–, author
        Injun / Jordan Abel.

Poems.
Previously published: Saskatoon, Sask. : JackPine Press, c2013.
ISBN 978-0-88922-977-8 (paperback)

        1. Visual poetry, Canadian (English). I. Title.

PS8601.B437I65 2016   C811'.6   C2015-908252-8

For the Indigenous peoples of the Americas

"It is better to take what does not belong to you
than to let it lie around neglected."

—MARK TWAIN

[CONTENTS]

[INJUN]

a)

he played injun in gods country
where boys proved themselves clean

dumb beasts who could cut fire
out of the whitest[1] sand

he played english across the trail
where girls turned plum wild

garlic and strained words
through the window of night

he spoke through numb lips and
breathed frontier[2]

b)

he heard snatches of comment
going up from the river bank

all them injuns is people first
and *besides for this buckskin*

why we even shoot at them
and *seems like a sign of warm*

dead as a horse friendship
and *time to pedal their eyes*

to lean out and say the truth[3]
all you injuns is just white keys

c)

some fearful heap
some crooked swell

bent towards him
and produced a pair

of nickel-plated pullers
a bull winder of

dirty tenderness[4]
that stiffened into

that low-brow ice
that dead injun game

d)

he confessed over a pitch fire
two yards of bright luck

packed through a mangy boil
the antipathy of peaceable hills

going crazy over that injun smell
downwind from the storm

that bucked gold[5] and water
right into a ribbon of domestics

a reserve[6] of gas feather camps
dusted straight into the big kill

e)

no talk of rain that night
only concern for smoke

where fire found a home
from a knife drop silence[7]

that some might consider
just part of a dream

driven through tent flaps
and fared into his eyes

his stained altar of ease
straight walking the tick

f)

faces in their blankets
trigger fingers in their pockets

one straight trail gone district
gold and bad as a trace

if they had dreamed of nights
if they had eyes over fists

no free knotted nevada
in the pockets of soldiers

or grubbed up injuns
in the glean of discovery[8]

g)

    injuns in a heap
spring   boiled[9] over

lanterns buried
light against   day

old rifle   old trip
    the doubt outlasted

just cattle dying
a   promise of appetite

of one man owned

h)

who slanted[10] their memories
on   the backs of lids

who breathed on granite
without the   straight

who   squared their mines
bearing down on grubstake

who talked the signs
through   call and country

who   kept their dreams
in some scrape   town

i)

pockets filled   with knives
the camp fixed to a clasp

   a two-year-old   one eye
closed and sideways glancing

a licked   glass of jelly
bordering[11] an artful   territory[12]

a partial injun tongue
steady in an old mans fingers

blankets   over tender feet

j)

if prayers were   tolerable
        if money[13] shook like rattlers

trouble now   up   in the air
concerns over missing   knives

        after all *if a fella dont shoot*
no one man   can change him

because *a man can be anybody*
        except   little

even snakes are more vital
even bandages   wash away

k)

just the warpath[14]
just the all time disgust

  ringing rescue
  acts for the boys and
  injuns for the nights

all misdeeds at the milk house
all heap shoots by the sagebrush

  all the grub is somewhere
  down in the hungry bellies

of drunks all the dog cries
  are announced
  at the back door

l)

all day for a dollar
       mixing   mineral land[15]
       with the real thing

you can see it for yourself
       lets play   injun
and clean ourselves
      off the   land

same old   gun handed business[16]
       served up

on the hunt tracks
       of strangers

m)

god   must love half
           caste daughters

      and the angry race
of bl   ue eyed   prospect[17] struck
           fair taints

that br   ought their peaceful skin
      unthinkingly to the summit

        as the heart
        of the morning

dragged across the   s   ky

n)

man   must track
                all far off boots

                and   cr   eep

                hazard into
                little squaw[18] talk

        that   part   of sparkling
kn   ife love that

        hates   the trouble
                        of rope

                        and the   letters
                of tow   ns

o)

injun s   mu st   hang

       straigh t
       bl ack arrows

       o ff their
       sh oulders

       an d be   th   ankf ul[19]
       and b e faithf ul
       a nd   be tr ustful

of si lver and
    lu ck

p)

g

cl   f

b loody[20]
te eth

o

kr   sc   out

p aleface   a
n a

c   r

s

si   lvertip

b

g   e

q)

s   a

bi   br

                              ct

l

                                    t

            os

    k   n   i

                  s

    n   sr

                xe

                      m

    as   m

            zn   ar

a

                        cr

        c   p

    h

r)

se ga re

p cɔ d

be ɔ v cu

cɹ ɐ8 ıɔ

cs so cl ar

ıɐ ɐu

la uz

n od

te ɯɯ

os se

kr si ɐ

ıu bi

ɯ8

sc na

me ᴚ x ʎ

ɹʞ əx ɯ8

əu f ɟ

sr ɹs

bɯ ʎ xɐ kr

na əu

me sɔ

na ıu

as bi si ɹʞ

so

mn u

əɟ

od n

po ɐl

zn ar

so cs

na ar cl cr ga

ɹɐ be

p cu ʌ ıq cɔ ɔ

ɐ8 d

əɹ əs

nd   g   e

p

c bi   v

b

cl ar

cs   jk

la

n   te

o

va kr   si

ni

sc   na

y

ne

sr   f

m xe kr

g

as bi

m

p

zn   ar

a s

cr g

ty c

p c

(s

re

p   esky   co   i   p
  i
cs   ar
                    sc   alped[21]

                              n
                n
        p eople   si

            y
    v ar mint

mg   kr   f ort

i njun

                bi
            k in   o   p o

                        pd
    ga   co lonel

                cu

                                        (1

```
        th e   d ay ki      cks up
   lik     e a pa   ck of wo        lves
      o          n the      c      ut


     bu    zza       rds
        ar    e fin        e b    irds
     th     at a   re fo       ol  ed
   b     y m   y   re        dsk in
                    sc ent


   no   k    een spir          it       ed
     wh   ite          fl        esh


            sh     ak        ing tr   ails
    i   n the w    alk         lig    ht


       no    le    ve        led ri   fle
     i    n t   he w        oods
        wh    ere    i sl        ept


   al     ong    tow      ards
      th    e           d   ay


                                    (n
```

b a   ck to th   e bl o   ody gor ge

t   o   t   h   at m ad
  pa le   fac   e se   tt ler

  bur n   ing g   ood   fe l low
           de   ad h ea   ps

           in   rat tles   na ke

  cou   nt   r   y²³

              ba   ck
        to   th   e

              fo   l ks
          i   c all

      br   ot her   a   nd
sw ee   t   he   ar   t
        a nd   suc   h

                                    (ʌ

            i s   ee   t he cl   ear
        m   ad st rea   m

    bo   di   es
ar e ma   de
fr   om t   he we st[24]

        b r   av   e
        chr   is t ian tr ibes

            c   amps o   f
                ho   st il e
                hun   ter s lea rni   ng
                 t o lo v   e

                    wi   nd fi   el ds
            o f

            wo rk ski   n
tr e m   or   s
        ch asi   ng th e   sc a   lp

                                        (W

```
           bl    ac  k hair     frontie     r
           i       hea  r y   ou   r
       d   ead he    ro     es

   th is  bu  rde  n
    sta  lk     ed    throu  gh
    the i    njun   g  ras  s

       thi    s      a    xe
          wh    ips  sca     rs
          i   nt    o dar      k
          f     ac   es

       th    is ha   lf br        ee  d²⁵
          g   rit ca   rri    es

          u  s    u    nwav    e   rin  g
            in to the sle      dg  e
            h   a  mme   r da          wn

                                    (x
```

        i   nto the hollow   r   ampage
            int   o the   flagstaff br   each

   wit   h my w   inter confiden   ce
   boi   ling the ambush fa   ith[26]

like eve   ry   fire
        q   uickened pa   ce

            th   e abandon   e   d
            b   o   omv   ille ban   k

            the r   ose ho   te l
            b   uck   ling wit   h shar   es

            of wh   ite h eat
            tr   apped i   n

   b y the lu   cky bo   die s
            of yu   ma

                                        (Á

a s   tea mham mer
    p lay of p rinci ples
     a   n d w earines s

          an   interc our se
          of title[27] and po   ssess i o n[28]

th at br eak s
th e fing ers

          o f the riv er

and lea ves m e
wild ey ed and
e xasp   erat e   d

          by the mu d

          sp ru ng sh or e

                                        (z

[NOTES]

1)

himself clean strain that night, the **whitest** little Injun on the reservati
s along the Missouri River had the **whitest** lot of officers that it was eve
at is spirit. He smiled, showing the **whitest** and evenest teeth. Such ext
'Jerry wants to talk to you. He's the **whitest** of the lot, if you can call tha
d not observe that his teeth are the **whitest**, evenest." "'They make them
oked from face to face. "You're the **whitest** bunch—I'd like to know—
1't much just to look at, but he's the **whitest** man I ever knew. You wait
ill you see Blanco Sol! Bar one, the **whitest**, biggest, strongest, fastest,
el rolls, pure, clean, and sweet, the **whitest** and finest in the world! Am
l her, anyway. Monty Price was the **whitest** man I ever knew. There's N
me. Al Auchincloss always was the **whitest** an' squarest man in this sh
An' Coles swore thet Wade was the **whitest** man he ever knew. Heart of
alousy and be half decent. He's the **whitest** man I ever knew. "Now list
te of Colorado you're known as the **whitest** of the white. Your name's a
with startlin' truth. Wade was the **whitest** man I ever knew. He had a

ıge. San Antonio at this time was a **frontier** village, with a mixed popu
s and asked none in return. In this **frontier** village at a late hour one ni
 passing glance. Interesting as this **frontier** life was to the young man,
the work before them. There was a **frontier** on the south and west of ov
·edit due for guarding this western **frontier** against the Indians and ma
ıe soil, as a boy the guardian of the **frontier** was expert in the use of firc
ıds. In the use of that arbiter of the **frontier**, the six-shooter, they were ;
near to hear him. His years on the **frontier** were rich in experience, th·
ıve it to the stronger republic. This **frontier** on the south has undergon
unties in Texas while it was yet the **frontier**, and by industry and econc
n the early days usually graced the **frontier** towns with their presence.
ıinner said that he had been on the **frontier** some little time, and that t]
at the Ford was quite a pretentious **frontier** village of the squatter type
lassify him at a passing glance as a **frontier** gambler. As we turned awa
ern trail. On coming opposite that **frontier** village, Parent and I took t]
· another trail drover. Sutton was a **frontier** advocate, alike popular wit
d had grown into manhood on the **frontier**. Sponsilier was likewise plc
ıd herd. It was a unique posse. Old **frontier**smen, with patriarchal beaı

3)

id that there was a great amount of **truth** mingled with the humor. Son
l spectacle before him. Then as the **truth** gradually dawned upon him,
er children to fear God and tell the **truth**. My vigil was trying to one of
packs. That once, at least, I told the **truth**. Every mother's son of them
and they never shook me from the **truth** of it. I soon learned that robb
on your head if you're telling us the **truth**; only do as you're told, for we
ion to go: 'Son, if you've told us the **truth**, don't look back when you rid
gave him free license to call it. The **truth** is, I didn't pay any more atten
. Half the teamsters, good, honest, **truth**ful men as ever popped a whip
now everything. I must tell her the **truth**, and I'd hate to tell her we bu
l his ability to protect himself; and **truth** compels me to say that the ou

4)

man and never feel the violence or **tenderness** of passion till there con
," he declared, and there was more **tenderness** than hunger in his tone
h alternately held her with the soft **tenderness** of a mother and crushe(
depen's." There was a look of great **tenderness** in his eyes as he bent to
bered her husband now with more **tenderness**, more charity, than she
to conceal his yearning, homesick **tenderness**. But when he read the le
xpress more depth of feeling, more **tenderness**, if you please, Mr. Franc
wanted her in the old days, with a **tenderness**, an impulse to shield he
questioning faith in his protecting **tenderness**. CHAPTER FOURTEE

5)

ı Bud would have paid its weight in **gold** dust (if one may believe his wc
ag, heavy and grimed and knobby. **Gold** inside it, he knew without loo'
natch his astonishment. "Yeah. It's **gold**, all right. Old man Nelson's hc
uire around and see. But seein' the **gold** is found on the claim, and we'·
ıt it. Cash and Bud dumped all the **gold** into a pan, and weighed it out
fortunes go. It was probably all the **gold** Nelson had panned out in a co
hed in a scarlet blanket edged with **gold**, on which a silver gorget glitte
plumage, and give us to live for the **gold**en moment." "And for the futu
bent timidly and kissed the rough **gold** circlet where my lips had reste
ı. Blueberry scrub, already turning **gold** and crimson, grew sparsely on
ı, and lay down prone, smooth and **gold**en, and shining like a sleek par
ımed in a riot of azure, purple, and **gold** on every side were the lovely w
ıide were the lovely wild asters and **gold**en-rod; and no pretty garden sı
ıuing to smoke his pipe. Slowly the **gold**en-brown eyes of Butler contra

6)

now, Fairchild worked with all the **reserve** strength that was in him. H
:ed out. He seemed to draw upon a **reserve** strength, for he grew comp
nancy of the moment Lane lost his **reserve** and told her the truth of his
trouble and to protect her. Strong **reserve** force suddenly came to Mel
'ride, honor, love never smothered, **reserve** rooted in the very core of a
By the expenditure of his last bit of **reserve** strength he could make the
ed and helped; but she had found a **reserve** fund of strength, and her m
k figures. The I.W.W. had begun to **reserve** their fire, to shift their posi
'. Afternoon of that very day, at the **reserve** camp somewhere back ther
:rilous life. And I began to think of **reserve** powers of fortitude and enc
e soon discovered to be the natural **reserve** of women who did not live
)uane thanked him, conscious of a **reserve** and dignity that he could n

7)

on, then fear. In the quick ensuing **silence** Miss Longstreth rose white
nger," replied Duane. A significant **silence** ensued. "I charge Snecker w
vith a cough that broke the spell of **silence**, shuffled a couple of steps to
l in his cold, ringing speech. In the **silence**, both outside and inside the
way you'll let us." There was a long **silence**. "Well, you look a little like
i with warning hand commanding **silence**, Duane stepped softly forwa
He sank down, controlled himself, **silence**d a mounting exultation, the
and evil deeds. There was absolute **silence**. The outlaws were lined bacl
\-huh!" exclaimed Snake, in relief. **Silence** ensued then for a moment, i

8)

ours before she made an alarming **discovery**. Accompanied by her sist
ind intimate dreams, had been the **discovery** that Harve Riggs was on
to grow denser. She made another **discovery**. Ever since she had enter
· forced detention there or possible **discovery** by those outlaws suppos
garded with contempt for himself. **Discovery** of this particular dog car
aid Moore, once, in surprise at the **discovery**. "You're losing hope and
or it seemed so, and soon made the **discovery** that the sweet, pungent,
to our momentary humor was the **discovery** that he was as wild as a M
the sage on his back trail. With the **discovery** of Oldring's hidden cattl
a fine fire, without hurry or fear of **discovery**. After hard work that ha
had happened from the time of his **discovery** of the rustlers in the can
elieve I can claim credit of that last **discovery**—before you," Venters sa
ise. Some time before I had made a **discovery** that I imagined would be
nd not far from camp—a welcome **discovery**. Next day we broke camp
self to watch the valley I made the **discovery** that near me were six low

9)

rug store over there, with the hard-**boiled** hat on.' "The old man started
. There was only half a dozen hard-**boiled** eggs to the man, and I don't
g a pot lid, "that these birds are par**boiled** by this time. Bring me a fork
l on the platform nightly, the brine **boiled** and skimmed, until a perfec
which sprung the spruce blade and **boiled** the water to a foam, while ri
he ants' nest. Victoria's stomach is **boiled** red altogether, and so painfu
Belgian hare off of silver service or **boiled** jack-rabbit out of a coal-oil
eans in the corner of a blanket and **boiled** out a South American liquic
andwiches and a mug of hot coffee **boiled** with milk in it and sweetene

10)

ash looked up at him from under a **slanted** eye-brow. His lips had a
:up of coffee to cool it, his memory **slanted** back along the years when I
 vas not so fearsome, since sunlight **slanted** down into many a passage-
ng in their gaze, and her eyebrows **slanted** upward a bit at the outer
)ut forty rod of six-foot guard, and **slanted** so it'll shoot a fire right
isco paper spread before him. Jack **slanted** a glance or two toward the
The rock walls rose sheer, the roofs **slanted** rakishly, the signs scratche(
)ad daylight, though the sun's rays **slanted** in through the window;
rth any one's watching. A cigarette **slanted** from the corner of his boyi:
iry V stood, her camera once more **slanted** uselessly in her two
:dge of the cockpit, keeping an eye **slanted** toward the brush fringe.
g the polished propeller blade that **slanted** toward him; he fingered th(
rd, alighted running with his body **slanted** backwards and his lips smil
!" Mack Nolan laughed, and Casey **slanted** a look his way. "Thought I l(

11)

curves, delightfully white with the **bordering** of green on either side. H
. dim, wide streak, lighter than the **bordering** gray, wound down the va
overing that part of the wheat-field **bordering** the road he collected twe
nan. Fires of hell, in two long lines, **bordering** a barren, ghastly, hazy st
a strip of ground, higher than the **bordering** forest, which was compa
ar. Silently he sank into the bushes **bordering** the trail. He listened wit
iippewa glided into the low bushes **bordering** the creek. Legget followe

12)

irring across the line into Mexican **territory**. Madeline's sensibilities w
-center of several hundred miles of **territory**. On the main street there
d the boundary line of his hunting **territory**. The decision he made to t
the mouth of the river. A vast wild **territory**—a refuge for outlaws! Sor
ɔlieved that he was getting on safer **territory**. Twice he came to a wide t
ɔart of an outlaw, drifting into new **territory**. He passed on leisurely be
politics for a while, and of the vast **territory** west of the Pecos that seer
', when it's paid, you strike for new **territory**." "Thet might be wise," mι
ɔn whistled low. "An' leave for new **territory**?" repeated Snake Anson,
is hand to indicate a wide sweep of **territory**. "Me sick." Nas Ta Bega la
l another ball into Clammer's wide **territory**. The hit was of the high an
ormer excursions and entered new **territory**. Here the woods began to
ɔein' as how we won't be in redskin **territory** fer awhile yit, we kin hev ɑ
and started across country for new **territory** near Whitley's Peak. We r

13)

ut of Horton Thicket. I'll send you **money** in advance to pay for this w
fortune and knew how to save his **money**. He would have been a milli
fended on moral grounds. But vast **money**ed interests are at stake. One
r home port, a quarrel arose about **money** due the young giant, and in
be on the trail. Think, man, of the **money**—the gold! Millions spilled
d spent their all trying to raise the **money** to build the Union Pacific;
he Government could do but little **money**-raising with land-grants an
nd paid in one-quarter of that. The **money** went so swiftly that it opene
directors, believing that whatever **money** was to be made out of the U
those who hired out for reasonable **money** soon learned that others we
sted," replied Larry. "I've plenty of **money**," said Neale, "and what's mi
ainst the middle; they received the **money** from the stock sales and loa
sack in which Slingerland kept his **money** and few valuables, and the
t for him. The winning or losing of **money** was not of great moment. P

14)

got aplenty when Buck went on th' **warpath**, an they's hankerin' to git
n't go where I please I'll start on th' **warpath**. I won't buck the cavalry, t
:ing Sheldon as a "Shawnee" on the **warpath** while he dodged from one
it ain't no sign he's goin' to take the **warpath** immediately, if not soonei
tcher-knife he had and went on the **warpath**. He found the old fellow si
u know them Cochises ain't on the **warpath**? Them Injuns has been on
send me word before they take the **warpath**," mother observed reassui
topped Colorou from going on the **warpath**? It would have been simpl
'. "We didn't come over here on the **warpath**, and, if you hadn't got in s
ind make her believe they're on the **warpath**—say, I'll gamble she'd rur
ng like a duck. You can't make that **warpath** business stick, Clark—not
vould make a tame showing on the **warpath**, however much they migh
ld Hagar, Grant! She's right on the **warpath**, and then some. She'd like
) use asking the Injuns to go on the **warpath**," Gene announced disgus

15)

k, and by mining a little where his land was untillable, and farming a l
an caught him." "Bet you couldn't land him," chuckled Baumberger, b
ɔp—and that there makes mineral land of it, and as such, open to entr·
ut of covering up valuable mineral land on purpose. And he says the la
y innocent, too. It was: "'Expect to land big one to-night. Plenty of sma
ıs. He's a high authority—General Land Office Commissioner, if you p
all mineral deposits discovered on land after United States Patent ther·
pretty worried, chicken, over that land business." Miss Georgie offere
hanged my mind, and thought I'd land on you and trust to the lessons
nes to see Miss Georgie about this land business. She's wise to a lot of l
through a little gateway which the land left open by chance and was hi
:al. Mile upon mile, they chose the land that pleased them best; and by
l at the peace and the plenty in the land which lay around the bay. Cha
ion which made for trouble in that land where the primal instincts lay

16)

The kid said: 'None of your damn **business**!' That made Rawhide kind
ain, and told him to mind his own **business** and give advice when it w
king his part. But the Committee's **business** is to weed out the dangero
was a stranger to the better class of **business** men, and those who did k
give them a taste of this foot-tying **business**!" Dade went on tying the l
pulveda, with two vaqueros whose **business** it was to stop the depreda-
them right and left and doing a big **business** in beef, according to all
ae who would dismiss a distasteful **business** from his mind; and entere
ith the tale, made it his immediate **business** to find Jack and tell him tl
bad idea for you to mind your own **business**," Jack retorted bluntly. "Tl
anvenient to a man as full of ranch **business** as Dade Hunter found hin
iill snorted at their absolute lack of **business** instinct and let the subject
eason's calves was a matter of pure **business**, the manner in which that
lamned thing about this here lasso **business**, but I took 'em on that, anc
am," said Jack shortly. "But I've no **business** to be. Right now I don't be

17)

ıg. They were enthusiastic over the **prospect** and willing to bet all they
ntry. The burro was packed with a **prospect**or's outfit startlingly real iː
Applehead," Luck yelled when the "**prospect**orp" had turned a corner c
y camp not to feel jubilant over the **prospect** even of a brackish water-h
nk of the stories they tell about old **prospect**ors going crazy trying to fi
e he may be, if he has a title, or the **prospect** of one. Every one laughs a
he blood in him was a-jump at the **prospect** of leading his Heart's Desi
ant Burns was so cast down by the **prospect** that he made no attempt tᵢ
ɛt upon it. Val was so happy at the **prospect** of getting away from the tᵢ
ɛction of the wind, and of the faint **prospect** of rain. Cattle, driven fror
a special campaign train bearing a **prospect**ive President of our Unitec
ive-minute stop, during which the **prospect**ive President would stand
batim report of his statement. The **prospect**ive President had not done

ʾer and over on the slippery mat of **squaw**-carpet. And for that he was

men. Don't dare to mention even a **squaw** to me, or I'll pitch you clean

dians. He had smiled at the fat old **squaws** who had waddled docilely i

ʾ upon the least of these. While the **squaws** grinned and murmured Inc

folded, watching him gravely. The **squaws** pushed straggling locks fro

ioke-tanned, blanketed bucks and **squaws** and papooses; not made-up

ʾd bucks and those fat, stupid-eyed **squaws** and dirty papooses. With tl

picture. You tell me be homely old **squaw** like Mrs. Ghost-Dog, I be hc

i this job." "Why don't you make a **squaw**-man outa Dave?" Pink sugge

t a heart-twisting smile, but she's a **squaw** just the same. She's got the w

ika after the submissive manner of **squaws** toward the human male in

iaps for reasons of his own, "Sioux **squaw**." Ramone very wisely let his

an, a childless old man—or else a "**squaw**" man whose squaw has, pres

aside the barrier of race and take a **squaw** for his wife. He could not see

ʾe fire curled over his head, and his **squaw** crouched in the shadow liste

19)

I came in after dark, too tired to be **thankful** for anything save the opp
wn-bred and awkward in the open, **thankful**ly resigned to the Indian g
rs——" Lorraine blushed, and was **thankful** that her dad had not watcl
lowjacket, she supposed, would be **thankful**. She had started not more
ve to say the more you'll have to be **thankful** fur, mebby." "I was wonde
e thoughtful." She snuggled into it **thankful**ly. "I was cold." Vaughan t
his satisfaction was tempered with **thankful**ness that he was clever enc
led into his bed with a long sigh of **thankful**ness, though his conscienc
ne collars, and then stand hipshot, **thankful** for the brief rest. She saw
g and just stopped and stood there **thankful** that they had an excuse, b
lache, Starr would have swallowed **thankful**ly the dose. The murder, o'
led and taxied back down the field, **thankful** that the soil was sun-bake

20)

deck. McTee's jaws fell open, and a **bloody** froth bubbled to his lips; his
ind when he had noted the froth of **bloody** bubbles which stained the li
nouth within was not so red as the **bloody** hands of Mac Strann; and tl
nd they stood with hanging heads, **bloody** foam upon their breasts anc
of the skull and merely ploughed a **bloody** furrow through the mat of l
. He attempted to speak, but only a **bloody** froth came to his lips. That
i like a beast, his lips flecked with a **bloody** froth. That bull-dog grip wc
and are greedily devoured red and **bloody**, and but barely warm. A liz;
1 measured inch by inch across the **bloody** archives of the nation. The i
iead—perhaps she was thinking of **Bloody** Cunningham, and the Prov
irs there, no moon, no sun—only a **bloody** mist in the forest. For to tha
1 Johnson's Greens, had done their **bloody** business; where, in "The Sh;

21)

e, Loskiel." "The Mole must not be **scalped**," said Tahoontowhee softly
strayed or stolen; and of men, too, **scalped** since they left Wyoming, so
e poor fellow was killed and partly **scalped**, and one wounded. The Yel
ott, who lay there dead and already **scalped**, doubled up in the bed of a
wn. It was a reproach to us that we **scalped** our red enemies. No officer
ay.... I had rather be here dead and **scalped** than have had that happen
gns and symbols—a dead tree-cat, **scalped**, and full of arrows; a snake
nes-town had as yet discovered the **scalped** bodies of the Eries in the gl
d I. "Why?" "I have dreamed I was **scalped**, and my hair still grows." "
r and salt shot into his flesh, being **scalped** alive and a host of other Ind
ll see all your friends and relatives **scalped** and burned. Quick, your ar
be done safely I crawled out. I saw **scalped** and mutilated bodies every
ated bodies of their sisters, and the **scalped** and bleeding corpse of a ba

22)

er goes there I'll find Girty and his **redskin**s. If it's night when I get bac
surprised to find the woods full of **redskin**s. He spent the remainder o
nce, out of reach of the destructive **redskin**s. All the horses and cattle ₁
₂as burning fiercely. "That infernal **redskin** is going to do that again," e
₁ thing to do in the face of all those **redskin**s. It is almost certain death!
.. "Send men to the south wall. The **redskin**s are breakin' in where the ₁
fought before. Every shot went to a **redskin**'s heart, impelled by the po₁
f me, and every village I struck the **redskin**s would crowd round me ar
ith you an' your rantin', dog-eared **redskin**s!" cried Rea. "I've run agin
l a few articles of flannel. "Thievin' **redskin**s," he added, in explanation
arms. Ho! here comes the howlin' **redskin**s." Rea whipped out a bowi₁
meward bound." "I hate to tell this **redskin**," replied Rea. "He'll be like
₁des, outlaws an' hoss-thieves. The **redskin**s ain't so bad as they used t₁
₁ed the colonel. "How's that?" "The **redskin**s are keen to burn things." ₁

23)

e occasion of your arrival in a new **country** a little plain talk will be wl
)? Well, I declare! This is a glorious **country**; but not for such as you, de
hance." "Wal, kunnel, this is a free **country**," growled Metzar. "I can't l
cause you're new in this part of the **country**." "I've been here as long as
uld hardly have been found in that **country**. The entrance was a narrov
the marching band. Then, in open **country** they reduced their speed to
He was entering the rocky, rugged **country** which marked the approac
se you, will you go away, leave this **country**, and never come back?" "I'
. Stewart own the best horse in the **country**?" asked Madeline. Again s
another start. But, Majesty, in this **country** that's a good deal of mone}
1e men—the real men of your own **country**." "Alfred, I'm afraid there a

24)

:rest in the U. S. in general, and the **West** in particular. The papers are f
ot adjust herself to these queer free **West**ern' ways. Her brother had elo
little about this incomprehensible **West**. "Majesty, I must run down tc
tlemen. Wal, Stewart's not a native **West**erner, but he's my pick of the l;
esty, I reckon, bein' as you're in the **West** now, thet you must take thing
s are new to you, an' fer sake of the **West** I'll explain to you thet we dor
tle wind you'll sure feel it," said the **West**ern girl. Madeline replied that
was turning rose. To the south and **west** the sky was dark; but every mc
ure like it. There! Look to the south**west**, jest over thet farthest ridge." I
orch smokin' my pipe an' facin' the **west**." So the old cattleman talked c
unknown at home, and here in the **West** it began to allure and drive he

you mean Beasley?" "Shore. He's a **half-breed**. He was born in Magdal
nd all that had occurred. "Wal, the **half-breed** son-of-a-greaser!" ejacu
ster. You ought to be hanged—you **half-breed** greaser!" "I'll cut out yo
with my hands crossed while that **half-breed** thief—Oh, it's unbelieva
f it were a fixture. "Heah's to thet—**half-breed** Beasley an' his outfit!" C
piercing eyes off Beasley. "Wal, my **half-breed** greaser guest, it shore ro
ɔnty-six empty shells. An' the little **half-breed** had one empty shell an'
ɪt I do know there are bad Indians, **half-breed**s and outcasts, hiding in
ered what Presbrey had said about **half-breed**s. A little shock, inexplic
o's Shadd?" asked Shefford. "He's a **half-breed** Ute—bad Indian, outlav
ɔeable, but there were bad Indians, **half-breed**s, and outlaws that made
got news of Shadd—bad news. The **half-breed**'s cutting up rough. His ɡ
nd closer glance to distinguish the **half-breed**. At once he recognized i

26)

sion had set in: she had not enough **faith** to uphold the burden she had
ide of resistless utterance. "Loss of **faith** and name did not send me to
f you understood. Think. I had lost **faith**, hope. I set myself a great worl
I felt it would cost to save her some **faith** must come to me again.... My
1ave brought me hope again. Some **faith** must come, too. It was throug
ist marry him, accept the Mormon **faith**, and bring up my children as l
se I could not be quick to learn the **faith**. "I am not a sealed wife. But tl
s Ta Bega, remember I lost my own **faith**, and I have not yet learned you
Indian was the undermining of his **faith**. It was not humanity that sent
at burdened Joe Lake then. Joe was **faith**ful to a love for Fay Larkin, no
Herculean task. He had lost hope, **faith**. The thing was not possible. B

27)

in the Sacramento Valley. But land **title**s were so uncertain that in 185:
ad gained the camp its infelicitous **title**, were not permitted within he;
uchess"; another, who had won the **title** of "Mother Shipton"; and "Und
isive man, who earned that baleful **title** by his unfortunate mispronun
new by any other than this relative **title**; that he had ever existed as a se
1ad heard her call him by that filial **title**, or indeed anything more thar
oung woman's already long-drawn **title**.) "O you wicked thing!" "I am
·d to the Atlantic reader under that **title**. The sharply defined boundari
ilt the shanty for that purpose, lest **title**s should fall through, and we'd
· an intentional emphasizing of the **title** and of its distinction that bega
words in question were simply the **title** of an idle novel, and, of course
nguished stranger; above all, some **title**d member of the British nobilit

28)

ght of charter, the other by right of **possession**, he proposed that the tw
to the internal trade once in their **possession**, the whole country wou
ne mountains. He would then have **possession** of the trade, not merely
ic with white men had put them in **possession** of vessels of superior de
dea of, some time or other, getting **possession** of one of their islands as
proclaiming formally that he took **possession** of the country in the na
nd gallant appearance, and, taking **possession** of a point which comma
bout a hundred, had already taken **possession** of a point near which th
uffalo in its migrations. Their only **possession**s were horses, which the
edecessors of those found in actual **possession**, and who must long since
y. The weary travellers gladly took **possession** of the deserted log huts
orses, and a little of every article in **possession** of the party; a reward su
ed to him, and been the best in his **possession**, and that it had been sto

[APPENDIX]

The boys from the other herds—good men, too—kept shooting them into the water, and inside fifteen minutes' time we were in the big   Territory. Early the next morning I sent one of my boys out on the highest sand dune to   around and see what they were doing. As we passed out George turned back and apologized to the girls, saying, 'He's a good   . He proved himself clean strain that night, the whitest little   on the reservation. I had a little experience over east here, on the cut off from the Chisholm trail, a few years ago, that gave me all the   I want for some time to come. Well, that Texan wasn't looking for any particular   that day to give six of his own dear horses to. Mr.   came up to the fire and professed to be very friendly, shook hands, and spoke quite a number of words in English. The letter concluded with the   ction, in case we met any one, to conceal the ownership of the herd and its destination. He talked to the horses; he sang songs; he played   ; and that Christmas was a merry one, for the debt was paid and our little widow had beef to throw to the dogs. The message was from Mike Sutton, stating that a fourth member of the ring had arrived during the forenoon, accompanied by a United States marshal from the federal court at Omaha; that the officer was armed with an order of   ctive relief; that he had deputized thirty men whom Tolleston had gathered, and proposed taking possession of the two herds in question that afternoon. I was pained to hear that you and Tom have both gone plum hog-wild, drinking out of cowtracks and living on wild garlic and land-terrapin, just like   s. But when the hearing came up, Sutton placed Jim Reed and me in the witness-box, taking the stand later himself, and we showed that federal court that it had been buncoed out of an order of   ctive relief, in favor of the biggest set of ringsters that ever missed stretching hemp. "   -bit," "Man-afraid-of-his-horses," were some of the terms applied to us,—yet the practical plainsman knew enough to take warning from his dumb beast. Order was soon restored, when we proceeded, and shortly met the young German coming back up the road, who merely remarked on meeting us, "Dem   s shot at me." I'm going back to God's country,—back where there

ain't no   s." Honest   , I hope it will storm enough this winter
to try you out; just to see what kind of thoroughbreds you really are. No
use looking in Straw's commissary; he never has anything to eat;
        s won't go near his wagon." We freighted in from Dodge City with
bull teams, and it was sure the fringe of the frontier; no women—no
society—nothin' much except a fort, a lot of   s, and a few officials
with their wives and families. There was a look of great tenderness in
his eyes as he bent towards her and searched her face, but she was not
thinking of him, and at length he continued: "Fader Barnum, he's goin'
be here nex' Sonday for cheer up dem   . It ain't got the class of
them other pieces. While it's devised to suit the intellect of an   ,
perhaps; it ain't in the runnin' with The Holy City, which tune is the
sweetest and sacredest ever sung." Cloudy, bein' an   , has got his,
and I rise to state that I like that monologue, Silas on Fifth Avenoo,
better than all of 'em, which ain't nothin' ag'inst my judgment nor
yours. When he reaches man's real-estate the   agent ropes,
throws, and hog-ties him, then sends him East to be cultivated. Our
foot-runner likes that   war-dance best of all." She told herself that
it was brave of him to obey her   ctions so literally and to leave her
unembarrassed by his presence at this particular time. She says they
horned into some of the best   families, and she's one of the
'overs.'" There's something in the law that prevents   s gettin' in on
anything good, too; I don't rightly recollect what it is, but if it's legal
you can bet it's crooked. Naturally, I can't stand for this dirty, low-
browed   .' "'Well, he's an   ,' retorted Harman, 'and that's
enough. All I get a whack at now is   s, but I'm gradually beginnin'
to close in on the white teeth." "I thought you said you was practisin'
on   s." "   s is human. This here town had more heathens than
whites in it, and before we'd gone a block I seen a buck   and his
squaw idlin' along, lookin' into the store winders. The   pitched
some, but Mike eared him down finally, and when I come up I seen that
one side of the lad's face was swelled up something fearful. "Whoa!" I
told the   . When Mike produced a pair of nickel-plated nail-pull-
ers, Mr.   snorted like a sea-lion, and it took both of us to hold him
down; but finally I tied his hair around the head-rest and we had him.
The   had pretty well wore himself out by this time, and when he
felt those ice-tongs he just stiffened out—an   's dead game that-
away; he won't make a holler when you hurt him. "   heap big
squaw!" I wheeled out a kind of sewing-machine; then I pedaled it
while Mike dug into that   's hangin' wall like he had a round of
holes to shoot before quittin'-time. It was just like I said, this   's

white keys was wore off short and looked like they needed something, so we laid ourselves out to supply the want. D'you know it's foot-racin' time with the   s?" They must of had three hundred head of horses, besides a big outfit of blankets, buckskin, baskets, and all the plunder that an   outfit travels with. I stepped out in front of our tent and throwed my hand to my forehead, shading my eyes—that's the   sign of friendship. The   s was in breech-cloths and moccasins, and, of course, they created no comment; but the sight of a half-nekked white man was something new to these people, and the first flash they got at Mike's fancy togs told 'em they'd once more fell a victim to the white man's wiles. All them   s done, was to come and look at Mike and feel of his legs and argue with one another. Seemed like a low-down trick to play on an   oo like her, and the more I studied it the warmer I got. I'm goin' to beat this   champeen, take my half of our winnin's, sell off the runty ones, and settle down." "You mean you're goin' to turn out with the   s?" I inquired, with my mouth open. Mike Butters could run too fast to be wasted among savages, and, besides, it's a terrible thing for a white man to marry an   . "All   s look alike—except one." And it impressed the other   s, too; they crowded up and studied it. "Mebbe it's because it's goin' to be my last race; mebbe it's because that   knows me and ain't scared of me. It was beautiful to watch those two men jockey for a start; the   was lean and hungry and mighty smart—but Mike was smarter still. With that them   s begun to speak. "He told me that he reckoned he was locoed, and always had been since a youngster, when the   s run in on them down at Frisbee, the time of the big 'killing.' He had formed a sort of antipathy for   s at that time, which he confessed he hadn't rightly been able to overcome. Then I looks carefuller and seen it wasn't no feather-duster at all—nothing but an   .' Them   s has been on their reservation for five years, peaceable, domesti-cated, and eating from the hand. 'You can talk as well as I can, and you're a going to tell us about this   killin'. Besides, the boys had more than they could manage,   s on three sides.   ctions, hear-ings and appeals, and now she was coming back, swearing she'd been "jobbed," the judge had been bought, and the jury corrupted. "It's only an   . The h   say that's w'ere hall the storm come from, bic-cause w'en the win' blow troo the Ass's Ear, look out! I guess maybe you ain't any more crazy over that   smell on yuh, than what I am—and that ain't any at all." Help yourself, kid—you ain't in no   camp now. "I was going to take off these dirty duds and wash some of the   smell off yuh. I'll tell the world straight, it's plumb cold and

snaky outside to-night, and you're pretty darn lucky to be here instead
of in some   camp where you'd have to bed down with a mess of
mangy dogs, most likely. I'll git me a radiator that don't boil like a
teakettle over a pitch fire, and load up with water and grub and gas, and
I'll find the   Jim mine, mebby. There's an old   been in the
habit of packin' in high grade in a lard bucket, and nobody's been able
to trail him and git back to tell about it. But I'd ruther go hunt the
Jim mine, Bill." And hills and chucks—say, don't talk to me about any
         packin' gold in a lard bucket. Casey asked the man why some one
didn't trail the   . The old buck—   Jim, they called him—was
an old she-bear. All the Indians were afraid of him and would hide
their faces in their blankets when he passed them on his way to the
gold, rather than be suspected by   Jim of any unwarranted inter-
est in his destination. A few had attempted to trail   Jim, but no
one had ever succeeded, because that part of Nevada had not had any
gold stampede, which the man declared would have come sure as fate
if   Jim's mine were ever uncovered. He said that   Jim lived
mostly in the Tippipah district. No free gold had ever been discovered
there, nor much gold of any kind; but   Jim certainly brought free
gold into Round Butte whenever he wanted grub. He dreamed nights
of trailing   Jim, and if he'd had any money to outfit for the venture
he surely would have gone straight to Nevada and to Round Butte.
However, he went among men with his ears wide open for gossip con-
cerning   Jim, and he gleaned bits of information that seemed to
confirm what his passenger up in the Yellowstone had told him. He
even met a man who knew   Jim.   Jim, he was told, had one
eye and a bad temper.   Jim nursed a grudge against the whites
because of that eye, and while he behaved himself nowadays, being old
and not very popular amongst his own people, it was taken for granted
that his trigger finger would never be paralyzed, and that a white man
need only furnish him a thin excuse and a fair chance to cover all traces
of the killing.   Jim would attend to the rest with great zeal. "That
old   don't travel long trails. And all   s are lazy.   Jim
prob-ly run across a pocket somewheres when he was hunting. Can't
be much of it—he'd bring in more at a time if there was, and be   -
rich. He wanted to hear a little more about   Jim. Not altogether
concerning   Jim, understand,— but local tidbits that might make
him a welcome companion to the old buck when he met him. It would
be just his grinning enemy Ill-luck on his trail again, if that light should
prove to be made by men hunting for   Jim and his mine. If they
were seeking   Jim, then he must find some way to head them off,

circumvent their plans with strategy of his own. There were striped silk shirts which made Casey grin and think how tickled   Jim would be with them,—or one or two of them; Casey had no intention of laying them all on the altar of diplomacy. And the next evening he tied the tent flaps carefully and fared forth with William to find the camp of   Jim and see if his dream would come true. He had not expected to walk straight into the camp of   Jim. But here was a one-eyed buck, and he was old, and he lived in the Tippipahs,—   Jim by all description. Casey had achieved the first part of his dream; he was making friends with   Jim. To find   Jim and get him to tell where his gold mine was had seemed fairly easy to Casey when he was driving stage elsewhere, and could only think about it. But when he sat on his haunches in the tepee, smoking with   Jim and conversing intermittently of such vital things as the prospect of rain that night, and the enforced delay in his journey because his pack mule was lame, speaking of gold mines in a properly disinterested and casual manner was not at all easy. As for medicine, he hadn't a drop, and if he had he did not know for certain what ailed   Jim.   Jim ate the jam, using a deadly looking knife and later his fingers, when the jam got low in the jar.   Jim did not want Casey; he wanted more jam. He took them to the tepee, and   Jim ate the complete contents of both cans and seemed disgruntled afterwards; so much so that he would not talk at all but smoked in brooding silence, staring with his one malevolent eye at the stained wall of the tepee. And that night   Jim was very sick. Next day however he was sufficiently recovered to want more jam. Casey filled his pockets with small cans and doled them out one by one and gossiped artfully while he watched   Jim eat pickles, India relish and jelly with absolute, inscrutable impartiality.   Jim ran his forefinger dexterously around the inside of a jelly glass and licked the finger with the nonchalance of a two-year-old.   Jim considered, his finger searching for more jelly. "White man no good for   , mebby. No place for   s no more.   Jim accepted a cigarette and smoked it, saying never a word.   Jim turned himself painfully on the blankets and regarded Casey steadily with his one suspicious eye.

      Jim called out vicious, Piute words. She stood there sullenly while   Jim berated her in the Indian tongue, and once she muttered a retort that made the old man's fingers go groping over the blankets for a weapon; whereat the young squaw laughed contemptuously and went out, sending Casey a side glance and a fleeting smile as full of coquetry as ever white woman could employ.   Jim muttered in Piute, or lay with his one eye closed.   Jim opened his eye suddenly, looked all around the tepee and then stared fixedly at Casey.

Jim fondled it evilly. He had not planned an exclusive jam diet for

Jim, therefore his supply was getting low. But at the tenderfoot camp was much more, enough to last   Jim to the border of the happy hunting grounds,—if he did not loiter too long upon the way. There was no telling how long   Jim would be able to eat jam, but Casey was a good gambler.   Jim laid the blade of his knife across the clasped hands.   god biteum. He made the trip almost half a day sooner than he had promised and went straight up to   Jim's camp with his load. "Me ketchum heap jam for   Jim. He unpacked William and gave her the things he had brought for   Jim, and returned with his camp outfit to the spring to think things over while he boiled himself a pot of coffee and fried bacon. Casey no longer wondered why

Jim insisted upon Indian dress for Lucy Lily. "Say, I never asked you about the darn mine, did I? I done my talkin' to   Jim. She accepted stolidly and together they buried   Jim, using his best blanket and not much ceremony. Hahnaga, however, brought two bottles of pickles and one jar of preserves which had outlasted   Jim's appetite, and put them in the grave with him, together with his knife and an old rifle and his pipe. That left Casey exactly where he had been before he found   Jim. She really did not know any more about

Jim's mine than did Casey. He did not see why, he said, the county of Nye should be let in for a lot of expense on   Jim's account, even if Jim had been killed. Then he suspects that it had something to do with

Jim's dying just when he did, and he has another count or two against the lantern and will tell you them, and back them with much argument, if you nag him into it. "The three darndest, orneriest, damndest things on earth," said Casey, as if he were intoning a text, "is a Ford, or a goat, or an   . I want to go hunt fer that mine of Jim's. I had talked with others about the mine of   Jim, and one man (who owned cattle and called mines a gamble) told me that he doubted the whole story. "You stake me to grub and a couple of burros an' let me go hunt the   Jim, and I'll locate yuh in on it when I find it. I never seen one of them lights till I started out to find   Jim's mine. And if you'd of saw   Jim, you'd of known same as I that it was the jam and the silk shirts that loosened him up. Bill was a good old scout, all right, but if he would grubstake Casey to go hunting the   Jim mine, then Bill had changed considerably. I felt much more certain that he would get into some scrape than I did that he would find the   Jim, and I was grinning inside when I went back to town; though there was a bit of envy in the smile,—one must always envy the man who keeps his dreams through all the years and banks on them to the end. They never showed more than slits of eyes beneath their drooping lids, yet they never missed seeing whatever there was to see, and taking advantage of every absent-minded moment when Casey was thinking of the Jim, perhaps. And when he set out again he went straight on to the old stone hut where   Jim had camped. He wanted to start his search from the point where   Jim had started, and he had rather a plausible reason for doing so.   Jim was an Indian of the old school, and the old school did a great deal of its talking by signs. That's the way he got his bearings; just remembering the unguarded motion of Jim's grimy hand and adding thereto his superficial knowledge of the country and his own estimate of what an old fellow like Jim could call a long journey. For the first time since he first heard of the   Jim gold mine, Casey felt that he was really "squared away" to the search. As he sat there blowing his unhurried breath upon a blue granite cup of coffee to cool it, his memory slanted back along the years when he had said that some day he would go and hunt for the   Jim mine that was so rich a ten-pound lard bucket full of the ore had been known to yield five hundred dollars' worth of gold. If it's huntin' the   Jim they're after, the quicker they scrape the sut off them dingbats and git outa here, the healthier they'll ride. With Babe in his arms he told her, too, about his coming out to hunt the   Jim mine. "Casey Ryan," the Little Woman began with her usual abruptness one evening, when she was able to walk as far as the mine and back without feeling; the effect of the exercise, but was still nursing a bandaged right hand; "Casey Ryan, tell me again just what old   Jim looked like." I merely need a fair description now of   Jim, to feel tolerably certain that I do or do not know something about the location of that mine." So Casey cooked supper, washed the dishes and helped Babe into her pyjamas; then he let her kneel restively in his lap while she said her prayers, and told her a story while he rocked her to sleep—it was a funny, Caseyish story about a bear, but we haven't time for it now— before he attempted to ask the Little Woman again what she meant by her mysterious curiosity concerning   Jim. "   Jim, that was— couldn't be anybody else!" "I've been waitin' a good many years for a look at that   Jim gold." Casey went away to his camp and lay awake a long time, not thinking about the   Jim mine, if you please, but wondering what he had done to make the Little Woman give him hell about his biscuits. Her opinion of him had become vital to Casey; more vital than the   Jim mine, even. In the hiding Jim had done his share, too. So they went hunting through the Tip-

pipahs for the mine of   Jim. In their wanderings she led the way
into the old camp of   Jim. "Snakes like   s. It was all very well
to explain missing horses by the conjecture that the   s must have
got them, but Buddy happened to miss old Rattler with the others. "I
told you, you can't change an   by learning him to eat with a knife
and fork," he added. I wish now," He blurted unthinkingly, "that I
hadn't killed the   that stole Rattler." If   s take in after me, the
gun's so I can shoot. And a feller don't shoot up in the air—and if an
          is hunting trouble he oughta expect that maybe he might get shot
sometime. But   s are different. You kill rattlers, and they ain't as
mean as   s. Mother always stuck to it that   s were God's crea-
tures—which brought Buddy squarely against the incredible
assumption that God must love them. D'you remember dragging into
camp on the summit one time when you was about twelve years old—
been hidin' out from   s about three days? Remember the time I
rode down and stayed over night at yore place, the time Bill Nye come
down from his prospect hole up in the Snowies, bringin' word the
          s was up again?" "Pop, you're about as appreciative as a buck
          ." Only one   ction did he lay upon the Happy Family. And
now he's   -giver. It was almost exactly like fighting   s, like
Uncle Gee-gee told about when he wasn't cross. Because his paternal
ancestry went back, and back to no one knows where among the race
of blue eyes and fair skin, the Indians repudiated relationship with
him, and called him white man—though they also spoke of him
unthinkingly as "Good   ." Because old Wolfbelly himself would
grudgingly admit under pressure that the mother of Grant had been
the half-caste daughter of Wolfbelly's sister, white men remembered
the taint when they were angry, and called him   . An'—I guess I
needn't ask yuh—be good to him. He ain't got anybody—not a soul—
          s don't count. "Want another drink, Good   ?" You no killum,
Good   ." "I told her, cross my heart, this morning that the   s
are peaceful now. I said Good   was the only one that's danger-
ous—oh, I sure did throw a good stiff load, all right!" "Good   , him
all time heap kay bueno," she stated emphatically, her sloe black eyes
fixed unwaveringly upon Phoebe's face to see if the stab was effective.
"Good   come Hartley, all time drunk likum pig. Squaws cry—
Viney cry—Good   "—Hagar paused here for greater
effect—"makum horse all time buck—ridum in wikiup—Hagar wik-
iup—all time breakum—no can fix that wikiup. Good   , hee-e-ap
kay bueno!" "Good   all same mebbyso yo' boy Grant, hee-ee-eap
kay bueno. Good   Grant all time DEBBIL!" It was at this point

that Donny slipped away to report that "Mamma and old Hagar are scrappin' over Good   again," and told with glee the tale of his misdeeds as recounted by the squaw. "Good   Grant, mebbyso home Hartley," she admitted reluctantly, as if she would have been pleased to prove Hagar a liar in all things. "Me thinkum no drunk. Good   Grant no heap yell, no shoot all time—mebbyso no drunk. 'Good   kay bueno. You say: 'Good   , him all time heap bueno.' Say: 'Good   no drunk, no heap shoot, no heap yell—all time bueno.'" Good   hee-eeap kay bueno! "What's the joke, Good   ? "There's no use asking the   s to go on the warpath," Gene announced disgustedly, coming out upon the porch where the rest of the boys were foregathered, waiting for the ringing tattoo upon the iron triangle just outside the back door which would be the supper summons. We don't need the   s. "Good   might do the rescue act and square himself with her for what happened at the milk-house," Wally suggested dryly. Makum   lazy. "Them grub all gone, them   s mebbyso ketchum hungry belly." "That's the   of it—I know YOU! Screech-owl—huh! Good   went after it with a gun, and I guess they mixed, all right, and he got the worst of it. Good   's scared clean off the ranch—you can see that for yourself. That's the   of it. And say," he added, with a return of his good-natured grin, "it looks like you and Good   didn't get acquainted yesterday. "Bothered much with   s?" "Yo' Good   —me likum for talk yo'." Good   —" Good   knows one of 'em." "Then," he added with slow emphasis, "if they don't go, after—say twenty-four hours' notice—why, we'll proceed to serve an   ction." You can get an   ction, and—" We can serve an   ction—" "   's on top," he diagnosed sententiously after a minute. "Baumberger," he said cheer-lessly, "was still talking   ction when I left, but—" He flung out his hand contemptuously. "He's got the   look in his eyes t'-day. "Good   says someone on the bluff took a shot at him when he was coming to the stable. I've stood for hours peeking out a knot-hole in the wall, with that same old shotgun Donny got hold of, ready to shoot the first   that stuck his nose from behind a rock." MUM will scare YOU, if there's any more of that let's-play-   business going on around this ranch. "   Charlie would hunt tracks all day for a dollar or two; only he'd make tracks just to prove himself the real goods." Good   him kill Man-that-coughs. "Yo' thinkum Good   love yo', meb-byso." Good   go all time Squaw-talk-far-off. Good   ka-a-ay bueno. "Good   boot make track, Squaw-talk-far-off little shoe make track. "Squaw-talk-far-off sabe Good   killum Man-that-

coughs, mebbyso," she hazarded, watching Good Indian's face
cunningly to see if the guess struck close to the truth. I'll bet you never
got an   ction against those eight men," she hazarded, leaning
toward him with her eyes sparkling as the subject absorbed all her
thoughts. "Good   makeum track all same boot. Seeum Good
      creep, creep in bushes, all time Man-that-coughs be heap kill. Yo'
buy hair, buy knife, mebbyso me no tell me seeum Good   . Me tell,
Good   go for jail; mebbyso killum rope." "Yo' no like for Good
      be killum rope," she chuckled. No trouble come Good   . No
ketchum, me tell sheriff mans Good   all time killum Man-that-
coughs." No trouble come Good   . I told him to kill you, you lying,
renegade   —and if he couldn't, I can! "Clark and I was going up to
the   camp," spoke up Gene. "Good   's the stuff, all right. You
know how things are going here, lately; and Perkins hates you since you
took the part of that peon he was beating up,—and, by the way, I saw
that same   at Don Andres' rancho. I sent a letter down by an
this morning to his pardner to come up and get him outa town before
he—But it's too late now. They've gone through a farce trial that'd make
the Digger   s ashamed of themselves; and they've condemned Jack
Allen, that's got more real manhood in his little finger than there is in
the dirty, lying carcasses of the whole damned outfit—they've con-
demned him to be hung! He gambles worse than an   , and never
has anything more than his riding outfit and the clothes on his back,
they tell me. When we fought   s, I don't believe it worried either
one of us to think we'd killed some. "They throned up their heads and
looked at me like I was wild   s, and I shooed 'em off—or tried to.
"Seems like the men that came here when there wasn't anything but
      s and animals, and built up the country outa raw material, ought
to have some say now about who's going to reap the harvest," he admit-
ted to Dade. "Only for the silver trimmings, you looked like a band of
warlike   s coming down on us with the sun at your back," laughed
Dade, as José swung down near him. I had one devil of a time with the
      , too, to make him disrespectful enough to throw a rope at me.
You ought to be thankful there's somebody on the lookout as faithful
as that   . "Diego—I forgot that   , Dade; and next to you, I
believe he's the best friend I've got on earth! ALL THIS WAR-TALK
ABOUT   S. If I was to say what I think, I'd say yuh can't never
trust an   —and shiny hair and eyes and slim build don't make 'em
no trustier. Applehead itched to tell her a few things about the social,
moral, intellectual and economic status of an "   squaw"—but there
was something in her eye, something in the quiver of her finely shaped

nostrils, in the straight black brows, that held his tongue quiet when he met her face to face. "   s are heap shy of meeting strangers. But that   had a heap of business off away from the ranch whilst you was in Los Angeles, Luck. "She's getting more   y every day of her life. We didn't see anything of her on the trail, but she could dodge us if she wanted to—she's   enough for that." ALL THIS WAR-TALK ABOUT   S. But what's gittin' to worry me, by cripes, is all this here war-talk about   s. "I betche there ain't been a   on the fight here sence hell was a tradin' post!" "We can't either," Applehead disputed, "because if Ramon takes a notion he'll steal fresh horses from the   s." "I thought you said he stood in with the   s," Weary spoke up from the ambling group, behind. "I can stand a decent dog barking at me, but so help me Josephine, I draw the line at   curs!" I'll pay the   s for what grass they eat. I'll bet they never throwed back any scout t' watch the back trail, In' they're in Navvy country now—whar they're purty tol'ble safe if they stand in with the   s. Er else they was held up fer some reason, 'cause them tracks is fresher a hull lot than what them was that passed the   ranch. "Ef them's   s, the bigger we stack up in camp the better. "Horses—and an   laying along the back of every one, most likely," Applehead returned grimly. "Nex' time old granny Furrman says   s t' this bunch, somebody oughta gag him." "'S jest like them dang   s!" "Take an   'n' he don't calc'late he's fightin' 'nless he's figgurin' on gittin' yuh cornered. Don't go bankin' on rocks bein' harmless—'cause every dang one's liable to have an   layin' on his belly behind it. Send back a shot or two if them   s gits too ambitious." "You fellers keep behind, now—and hold the   s back fer a minute er two," Applehead yelled while he set himself squarely in the saddle, gathered up his reins as though he were about to "top a bronk" and jabbed the spurs with a sudden savageness into Johnny's flanks. "They're   s— or there are   s in the bunch, at least," he told them after a moment. I saw an   peeking around the edge—to the south. "   s is tricky—" I know   s better than you do, Applehead. "Well, Lite, you keep your sights lined up on that   , then. But if this here's a trick t' git Luck, you KILL that   . He wouldn't go south, 'cause he could be traced among the   pueblos—they's a thousand eyes down, that way b'fore he'd git t' wild country. "We was all comin' on the jump, 'n' so was the   s; 'n' it was purty long range 'n' nobody but lite could hit 'n   t' save his soul. "Say, that red-white-'n'-blue ribbon sure looks fierce on that green dress—but I reckon blood will tell, even if it's   blood. Do yuh know anything about   ctions? "I believe I

may truthfully say that I understand the uses—and misuses—of
ctions, William. You just keep your eye on Brown, and if yuh can
slap him in the face with an   ction or anything, don't yuh get a
sudden attack uh politeness and let him slide. "Aw, I ain't meditating
no moonlight attack, Dilly—but the boys would sure love to do it if I
told 'em to get busy, and I reckon we could make a better job of it than
forty-nine   ctions and all kinds uh law sharps." "He'd plug me in
the back like an   if he thought he could get off with it. "I can take
the   s back," he conceded, "and worry along somehow without
them. I've got to have some whites to fill the foreground, if I give up the
       s; or else I quit Western stuff altogether. I've been stalling along
and keeping the best of the bucks in the foreground, and letting these
said riders lope in and out of scenes and pile off and go to shooting soon
as the camera picks them up, but with the   s gone, the whites won't
get by. "Maybe you have noticed that when there was any real riding,
I've had the   s do it. You'll have to take the   s back; nobody
else can handle the touch-me-not devils. And take these   s home,
and then get out after your riders. Some of the four-flushers I was
cursed with in the company,—because they were cheap and I had to
balance up what I was paying the   s,—they kept eyeing that bluff
where I said I'd come down with the coach, and betting I wouldn't, and
talking off in corners about me just stalling. We can't afford a lawsuit,
these hard times—and   ctions tying up the releases, and damages
to pay when the thing's thrashed out in court. "And my car ought to
bring three or four thousand,—if I can find the man that tried to buy it
a month or so before I took the   s back. She's got the ways of the
       to the marrow of her bones, and I'll bet right now if you were to
shake her hard enough, you'd jingle a knife out of her clothes." But
since Lorraine had not told her father anything about it, his   ction
could not have anything to do with the unreliability of the horse. And
right out in the open—live like an   for a year or two. "Wasn't them
       s?" he wanted to know, and his voice showed some anxiety. "Say,
f'r cat's sake, keep a watch out for   s and leave me alone! "Fat
chance we got of godding over   s this close to a town! There ain't
an   on earth could face that." Now you fly into   country
without so much as a sharp idea. "I know   s. The Navajos have got
a Thunder Bird mixed up in their religion, and I guess maybe these
       s will have, too. "Unless we take up a collection amongst the
       s cached out in the brush," he grinned ruefully to himself. So I
had to catch an   and make him take a note to the nearest station
for gas, and wait till he got back with some. I'd have sent word on to

you, but I was in such a darned hurry I forgot—and the   s were all
scared stiff, and it was only by making them understand I wanted water
for the Bird, and nothing else would do." With all this publicity, and
the   name—say, it's a cinch, bo! "Us, we been gawdin' amongst the
          s," he stated loftily. He put up at a cheap place on San Pedro Street,
with his car in the garage next door and a five-dollar tip in the palm of
a rat-faced mechanic with Casey's   ction to clean 'er dingbats and
keep other people away. To Arizona it seemed as if this last   ction
were personal advice. I hid in some bulrushes and waited. Pretty soon
along comes three   s, and when they saw where I had taken to the
water they stopped and held a short pow-wow. The last   did not
sink. I saw the   crawl up on the drift. If I can ever get a shot at any
of 'em I'll give up   s and go farmin'. "That stuff I picked up round
an   camp. "What can an   hunter say to amuse the belle of the
border?" "Hostile   s wouldn't show themselves like that. "   s.
Well, Betty, hostile   s are hidin' and waitin' fer you in them high
rushes right where you were makin' fer," said Wetzel. "Betty, I wanted
to tell you to stay close like to the house, fer this feller Miller has been
layin' traps fer you, and the   s is on the war-path. I have to report
that Girty, with four hundred   s and two hundred Britishers, are
on the way to Ft. Henry." Knowin' it's all up with me I deserted my post
when I heard the   s choppin' on the fence where it was on fire last
night. "I hated to run, Betty, but I waited and waited and nobody came,
and the   s was getting' in. They'll find dead   s in piles out
there. That was the wust   scrap I ever saw. All you'd had to do was
to drag the dead   s aside and give him elbow room." "Papa, when
shall I be big enough to fight bars and bufflers and   s?" The boys
visit the cave on Saturday afternoons and play "   s." "We saw your
fire blazin' through the twilight, an' came up just in time to see the
          s make off." Likely he expected those   s to show up a day or
two ago. I've a mind it's some slick white fellar, with   s backin'
him." An' the fellar steps as light as an   ." One, two, three, shad-
ows—   s!" "It's Wetzel, an' it means   s!" The words were
"   s! "Any   sign?" continued Jonathan, pushing toward his
companion the knapsack of eatables he had brought from the settle-
ment. I don't know Bing; but I've seen some of his   s an' they
remember me." We never tackled as bad a gang as his'n; they're all
experienced woodsmen, old fighters, an' desperate, outlawed as they be
by   s an' whites. When the   s are all gone where'll be our
work?" "I want to drink with that ther'   killer. The little man
threw up his cap, whooped, and addressed himself to Jonathan: "   -

killer, bad man of the border, will you drink with a jolly old tar from England?" He's slicker on a trail than any other   on the border, unless mebbe it's old Wingenund, the Huron. It was more luck than sense that we run into those   s with the hosses. Wetzel knelt and closely examined the footprint; "Yes, a woman's, an' no   ." "She's suddenly discovered somethin',   s, hoss-thieves, the Fort Henry traitor, or mebbe, an' most likely, some plottin'. But if he hasn't shaken Fort Henry by now, his career'll end mighty sudden, an' his bad trails stop short on the hillside among the graves, for Eb will always give outlaws or   s decent burial." "   s all around; I guess I'd better be makin' tracks," Jonathan said to himself, peering out to learn if Wetzel was still under cover. "I tell ye, Brandt, I ain't agoin' against this   ," Legget was saying positively. "All   vanity and pride." "It's   ways, an' we can't do nothin' to change 'em."   s is   s. "Mebbe he's waitin' for some   band," suggested Jonathan. "Suppose we run into some of these   s?" Buzzards are fine birds, most particular birds, as won't eat nothin' but flesh, an' white man or   is pie fer 'em." The redskin scents somethin' in the woods, an' ther's an   I never seed fooled. I can tell, 'cept at this season, by the way they whistle an' act in the woods, if there's been any   s along the trails." Thet's an   , an' he looks too quiet an' keen to suit me. See that   knock up a leveled rifle." Thet   guard, 'afore he moved, kept us from seein' her." "I see two   s sneakin' off into the woods, an' here comes thet guard. I ain't seen many keener   s. Legget'll send thet   back, an' mebbe more'n him. With a couple of   s guardin' thet spot, he'll think he's safe.   s get sleepy along towards day. An' he had to get an   to help him, fer she kicked like a spirited little filly. If they don't suspicion us, when the right moment comes you shoot Brandt, yell louder'n you ever did afore, leap amongst 'em, an' cut down the first   thet's near you on your way to Helen. But I was a mad an' bloody   hater, so I never let her know till I seen it was too late. He hed the   s slashin' each other like a pack of wolves round a buck." "He's a keen   ." We've   s here, an' ought to be a match fer two men." "He'd better have learned to walk light as an   before he took to outlawin'," said the borderman in disdain. "Air you goin' to live like an   all your days, Milt Dale?" she queried, sharply. "Honest   ," she responded. "Wal, you're more of an   than me," he replied, shaking his head. "Honest   , I'm glad—glad for his father's sake, for his own, and for yours. "Shore, if I ain't losin' my eyes, I seen an   with a red blanket," said Lassiter. Bo Stranathan bawled: "Wull,   s, hyar's were we do 'em. "Run, you   , run!" bawled Bo.

Howsumever, I've knowed   s who are good fellows, and there's no tellin'. "Well, lad, where you're goin' seein'   s ain't a matter of ·choice. "He's a traitor, and Jim and George Girty, his brothers, are p'isin rattlesnake   s. He's all the time on the lookout to capture white wimen to take to his   teepee. "Why, lad, the Village of Peace, as the   s call it, is right in the midst of that   country. The   s hev swarmed down on it time and ag'in, but they hev never burned it. Eb Zane's got but a few men, yet he kin handle 'em some, an' with such scouts as Jack Zane and Wetzel, he allus knows what's goin' on among the   s." Wetzel is an   -killer. He don't hang round the settlement 'cept when the   s are up, an' nobody sees him much. Fer instance, I've hearn of settlers gettin' up in the mornin' an' findin' a couple of dead and scalped   s right in front of their cabins. We soon struck   sign, and then come on to a lot of the pesky varmints.
        mad—heap mad—kill paleface." She come to me at the fort, an' tells as how her folks hed been killed by   s, an' she wanted to git back to Pitt to meet her sweetheart.   s stick close to a white man that has turned ag'inst his own people, an' Jim Girty hain't ever been ketched. "Ugh! Paleface sleep—   wigwams—near setting sun." "Might jes' as well kick an'   . "They're good   s now," said Wetzel, pointing to the prostrate figures. Silvertip'll soon hev a lot of   s here." "Not much. I treed five   s, an' two got away," answered the hunter as he walked toward the fort. "Shawnee—chief—one—bad—   ," replied Tome, seriously. I got cheated outen her, but I've got you; arter I feed yer   preacher to ther buzzards mebbe ye'll larn to love me."   s sometimes foller up a buffalo trail, an' I want to be sure none of the varlets are chasin' that herd we saw to-day." "I seen   sign," said Wetzel. "   s, an' not fer away." The   s has taken one of these streams." Then we'll come back here an' talk over what the fish has to say about the   s." I'll allow   s is bad enough; but I never hearn tell of one abusin' a white woman, as mayhap you mean.   s marry white women sometimes; kill an' scalp 'em often, but that's all. You might think they was chasin' a hawk, or king-birds were arter 'em, but thet fuss they're makin' is because they see   s." "Paleface brave—like   chief. "No, I ain't a Christian, an' I am a killer of   s," said Wetzel, and his deep voice had a strange tremor. I'll allow, hatin'   s as I do, is no reason you oughtn't to try an' convert 'em. These   s won't allow this Village of Peace here with its big fields of corn, an' shops an' workin' redskins. You're only sacrificin' your Chris- tian   s." The   s are mad clear through, an' I ain't sayin' I've tried to quiet 'em any. They might let them go back to the tribes, but

'pears to me these good   s won't go. He had ten   s with him,
an' presently they all made fer the west. I found the warm bodies of Joe
and thet   girl, Winds. 'Pears to me they're foolish to hold service
in the face of all those riled   s." By gum! who's that   stalkin'
over from the hostile bunch. Hev you seen any   Christians round
here?" asked Girty, waving a heavy sledge-hammer. But you can't see
the   s from our side. "I reckon not, but this   ain't one," replied
Wetzel slowly. "   , are you a Christian?" hissed Wetzel. "   , my
back bears the scars of your braves' whips," hissed Wetzel, once more
advancing. "The   's all right," Jones remarked to Emett. Ain't y'u
an   , Jean Isbel? Hair black as my burros, dark face, sharp eyes—
you'd took him fer an   . He wore a belt round his middle an' thar
was a bowie-knife in it, carried like I've seen scouts an'   fighters
hev on the frontier in the 'seventies. Mebbe thet damn half-breed Isbel
is comin' some   on us." He'll take an ax, an' his guns, of course,
an' do some of his   sneakin' round to the back of Greaves's store....
I heerd him chewin' to himself, an' when I asked him what was eatin'
him he up an' growled he was goin' to quit this   fightin'. Too much
        ! But I don't like   tracks. "Wal, I'll gamble the shot thet killed
this meat was heerd by   s," blurted out Horn, as he deposited his
burden on the grass and whipped out his hunting-knife. "Horn, I
reckon you 'pear more set up about   s than usual," remarked Jones.
"Thet's no   , but I don't like the looks of how he's comin'." "How
many   s?" "G'wan out among thim Sooz   s an' be a dead hero,
thin," retorted Casey, as the cowboy stalked off to be alone in the
gloom. "Wal, I reckon them   s," drawled Red. An'   s is
        s." The   s an' me are friends." More 'n thet, you've got some—
some quality like an   's—thet you can feel but can't tell about. You
needn't be insulted, fer I know   s thet beat white men holler fer all
thet's noble. If I stayed around another winter near Allie Lee—with her
alone, fer thet trapper never set up before thet fire—I'd—why, Neale,
I'd ambush you like an   when you come back!" The   s are on
the rampage already. "The   s! "A white gal in   dress," said
another. An' I allus regarded them buffalo as   property. An' keep
one eye peeled fer   s!" An' we had hell wid the   s gittin' here.
Killed by   s!' But the caravan wuz attacked by   s. He stood
like an   , with the big muscles bulgin', an' his face was clean an'
dark, his eye like fire.... Thet hat ain't much, but, say, the buckle was an
        's I shot, an' I made the band when I was in jail in Yuma." He
quickened his pace, and as the flagstaff of the Boomville Hotel rose
before him in the little hollow, he seriously debated whether he had not

better go to the bank first, deposit his shares, and get a small advance on them to buy a new necktie or a "boiled shirt" in which to present himself to Miss Kitty; but, remembering that he had partly given his word to Demorest that he would keep his shares intact for the present, he abandoned this project, probably from the fact that his projected confidence with Kitty was already a violation of Demorest's   c- tions of secrecy, and his conscience was sufficiently burdened with that breach of faith. For Barker, in spite of his mistress's   ction, had no idea of taking what he couldn't pay for; he would keep the claim intact until something could be settled. I has been buggy ridin' with an orfi- cer who has killed   s real! His letter closed with an   ction of wariness in his intercourse with the natives, a subject on which Mr. Astor was justly sensible he could not be too earnest. The captain received the same   ctions that had been given to Captain Thorn of the Tonquin, of great caution and circumspection in his intercourse with the natives, and that he should not permit more than one or two to be on board at a time. The first crippling blow was the loss of the Tonquin, which clearly would not have happened, had Mr. Astor's ear- nest   ctions with regard to the natives been attended to.   s, you chump!" Them   s'll have pickets out looking for Hoppy's friends. Damn   s, anyhow!" "I never did much pot-shooting, 'cept agin   s; but I dunno—" He did not finish, for the strangers were almost at his elbow. "Not even"—Hicks had leveled a forefinger at Chino, and the cold eyes drove home the   ction as the steam-ham- mer drives the rivet—"not even your wife." The Boss got a clod o' river-mud spang in the eye, an' went off his limb like's he was trying to bust a bucking bronc' an' couldn't; and ol' Mary-go-round was shoot- ing off his gun on general principles, glarin' round wild-eyed an' like as if he saw a'   devil. He's got no title, in course, but if he gits there afore we do and takes possession it'll take fifty years o' lawing an'   ctioning to git him off. Now Comanches, they're an unfriendly people, 'bout the unfriendliest   s, 'cept 'Paches, a man can meet up with. We're pullin' out soon as   draws us some travelin' rations. "We'll see what kind of luck we have along this road,   -scouted. You take first watch,   ?" When all the shootin' was over an' you didn't come 'long, me and   did some scoutin' 'round. Then   , he found your heart was still beatin', so we lugged you up heah an' looked you over. Later,   , he went back for a look-see, but he ain't found hide nor hair of Anse—"   , he could still be out there now ... "What about you,   ?" "You a teacher,   ?" Thar's parts maybe even an   ain't seed neither. But a lot o' them officers now—they

come out here wi' biggety idears 'bout how t' handle   s, thinkin'
they knows all thar's t' be knowed 'bout fightin'—an' them never facin'
up to a Comanche in war paint, let alone huntin' 'Paches. But he knows
you think   , you live   , you eat   , you smell   when
you do. Johnny's meaner than a drunk   these days. I never had no
use for   s, but these here are peaceful cusses—iffen they don't
smell an Apache. It's worse'n an   war. You know, a fella who's
scouted an' hunted   s an' popped bush cattle, to say nothin' of
toppin' wild ones what can look like a nice quiet little pony one minute
an' have a belly full of bedsprings an' a sky touchin' back th' next—a
fella who's had him all that kinda experience an' a saddlebag full of
surprises in his time gits so he can smell a storm comin' 'fore th' first
cloud shows. Ride 'long without some   or bandido poppin' lead at
m'back. No   would have jus' shot him down an' not made sure he
was crow bait. Anyway we jus' kept on, with me tryin' to think iffen I
should   up to git th' drop on 'em or not. These   s run us in an'
as far as th' Old Man's concerned we're jus' what everybody claims we
is. Bein' soft with   s—Lord, I was sick of bein' his kind of son when
I went off with Howard. Th' Colonel, he saw what might be done out
here where it's a long ride between sheriffs an' th' army hadda think
'bout   s most of th' time—what army there still was in th' terri-
tory. Lutterfield, he don't look much, but he was runnin' in this country
with th'   s thirty years ago. "But you mustn't think that, either,
and be reckless," was the next.   ction. That's him lying in his
blanket and chinnin' a squaw." "Oh, he's rigged up   fashion, fust
rate, sir. "He's like an   ," he said. No   , anyhow. She's   ,
yu' know, and five years of married life hadn't learned her to toss flap-
jacks. And she whipped out one of them   medicine-stones,—first
one I ever seen,—and she clapped it on to my thumb, and it started in
right away." You'll equal an   if you keep on."

[SOURCES]

Adams, Andy, 1859–1935

    Cattle Brands: A Collection of Western Camp-Fire Stories
    The Log of a Cowboy: A Narrative of the Old Trail Days
    The Outlet
    Reed Anthony, Cowman: An Autobiography
    A Texas Matchmaker
    Wells Brothers: The Young Cattle Kings

Beach, Rex, 1877–1949

    The Barrier
    Going Some
    Heart of the Sunset
    Laughing Bill Hyde and Other Stories
    Pardners

Bower, B.M., 1871–1940

    Cabin Fever
    Casey Ryan
    Chip, of the Flying U
    Cow-Country
    Flying U Ranch
    The Flying U's Last Stand
    Good Indian
    The Gringos
    The Happy Family
    The Heritage of the Sioux
    Her Prairie Knight
    Jean of the Lazy A
    Lonesome Land
    The Lonesome Trail and Other Stories
    The Long Shadow
    The Lookout Man
    The Lure of the Dim Trails
    The Phantom Herd
    The Quirt

Skyrider
Starr, of the Desert
The Thunder Bird
The Trail of the White Mule
The Uphill Climb

Brand, Max, 1892–1944

Black Jack
Bull Hunter
Gunman's Reckoning
Harrigan
The Night Horseman
The Rangeland Avenger
Riders of the Silences
Ronicky Doone
The Seventh Man
Trailin'!
The Untamed
Way of the Lawless

Carnegie, David Wynford, 1871–1900

Spinifex and Sand

Chambers, Robert W., 1865–1933

The Hidden Children

Cooper, Courtney Ryley, 1886–1940

The Cross-Cut

Ellis, Edward S., 1840–1916

Two Boys in Wyoming; A Tale of Adventure

Grey, Zane, 1872–1939

Betty Zane

The Border Legion
The Call of the Canyon
The Day of the Beast
Desert Gold
The Desert of Wheat
Heritage of the Desert
The Last of the Plainsmen
The Last Trail
The Light of Western Stars
The Lone Star Ranger
The Man of the Forest
The Mysterious Rider
The Rainbow Trail
The Redheaded Outfield
Riders of the Purple Sage
The Rustlers of Pecos County
The Spirit of the Border
Tales of Lonely Trails
To the Last Man
The U.P. Trail
Wildfire
The Young Forester
The Young Pitcher

Gunnison, Charles A., 1861–1897

The Beautiful Eyes of Ysidria

Hall, Angelo, 1868–1922

Forty-One Thieves: A Tale of California

Harte, Bret, 1836–1902

Selected Stories of Bret Harte

Irving, Washington, 1783–1859

Astoria; or, Anecdotes of an Enterprise beyond the Rocky Mountains

King, Charles, 1844–1933

> *Sunset Pass; or, Running the Gauntlet through Apache Land*

McNeil, Everett, 1862–1929

> *The Cave of Gold: A Tale of California in '49*

Mulford, Clarence Edward, 1883–1956

> *Bar-20 Days*
> *Hopalong Cassidy's Rustler Round-Up*

Norris, Frank, 1870–1902

> *A Deal in Wheat and Other Stories of the New and Old West*

Norton, Andre, 1912–2005

> *Ride Proud, Rebel!*
> *Rebel Spurs*

Raine, William MacLeod, 1871–1954

> *Bucky O'Connor*

Wister, Owen, 1860–1938

> *The Jimmyjohn Boss and Other Stories*
> *The Virginian: A Horseman of the Plains*

[PROCESS]

Injun was constructed entirely from a source text comprised of 91 public domain western novels with a total length of just over ten thousand pages. Using CTRL+F, I searched the source text for the word "injun," a query that returned 509 results. After separating out each of the sentences that contained the word, I ended up with 26 print pages. I then cut up each page into a section of a long poem. Sometimes I would cut up a page into three- to five-word clusters. Sometimes I would cut up a page without looking. Sometimes I would rearrange the pieces until something sounded right. Sometimes I would just write down how the pieces fell together. *Injun* and the accompanying materials are the result of these methods.

[ACKNOWLEDGEMENTS]

My greatest thanks go out to Chelsea Novak, who, on many occasions during the writing of *Injun*, came home to find scraps of paper everywhere. Thank you for putting up with my methods.

Thank you so much to Daniel Zomparelli and Project Space for curating and producing *Arte Factum* and, subsequently, for providing a space for my first attempt at writing this project. Thanks to *Grain* magazine and rob mclennan for publishing an early section of *Injun*, and for being among the first believers. Many thanks to JackPine Press for the amazing support of the chapbook version of *Injun* and for hosting me in Saskatoon during what I assume was the coldest winter ever. And thank you to *Geist* for publishing pieces of this long poem and for all the support.

Thank you to everyone who provided me with feedback on this project, especially Ray Hsu for your endless encouragement. Thank you to Kevin Spenst, Karen Shklanka, Emily Davidson, and everyone in Shadow Poetry for helping me think through this piece.

All my thanks to Joanne Arnott for your tireless support and for wanting to know who was going to pick up all the paper I had thrown on the floor.

And, finally, thank you so much to Leanne Simpson, Neal McLeod, Erín Moure, and Ken Babstock for your amazing generosity and for believing in this work.

Jordan Abel is a Nisga'a writer from Vancouver. Currently he is pursuing a PhD at Simon Fraser University, where his research concentrates on the intersection between digital humanities and indigenous literary studies. Abel's creative work has recently been anthologized in the *Best Canadian Poetry in English* series (Tightrope), *The Land We Are: Artists and Writers Unsettle the Politics of Reconciliation* (Arbeiter Ring), and *The New Concrete: Visual Poetry in the 21st Century* (Hayward). Abel is the author of *Un/inhabited* and *The Place of Scraps* (winner of the Dorothy Livesay Poetry Prize and finalist for the Gerald Lampert Memorial Award).